Life at tr

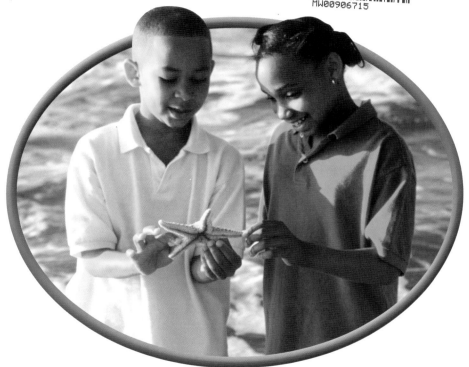

by Carrie Smith and Cameron Swain

I need to know these words.

beach

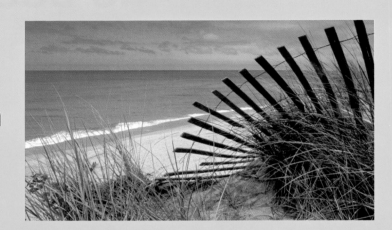

clam

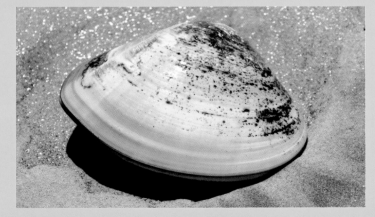

crab

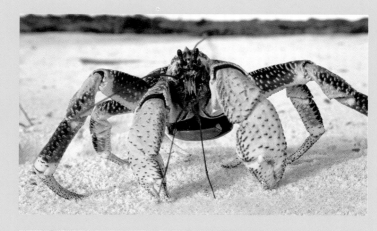

snail

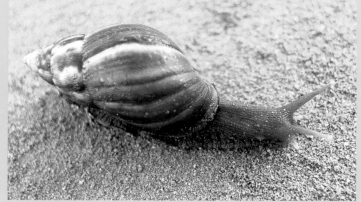

3

I see a snail.

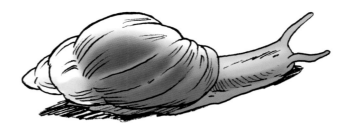

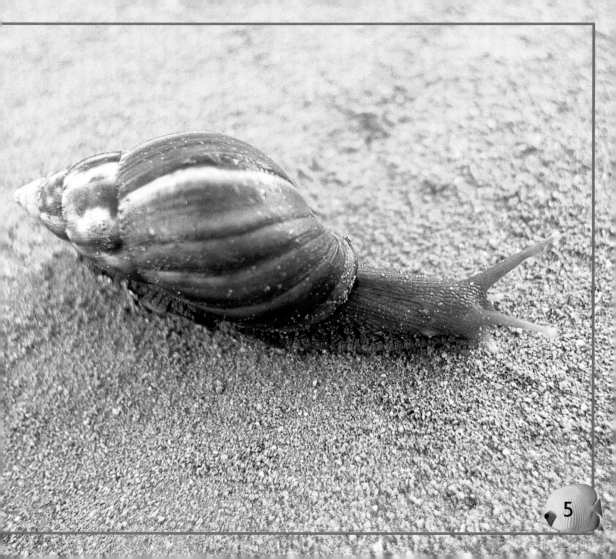

I see a clam.

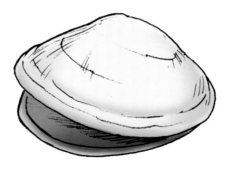

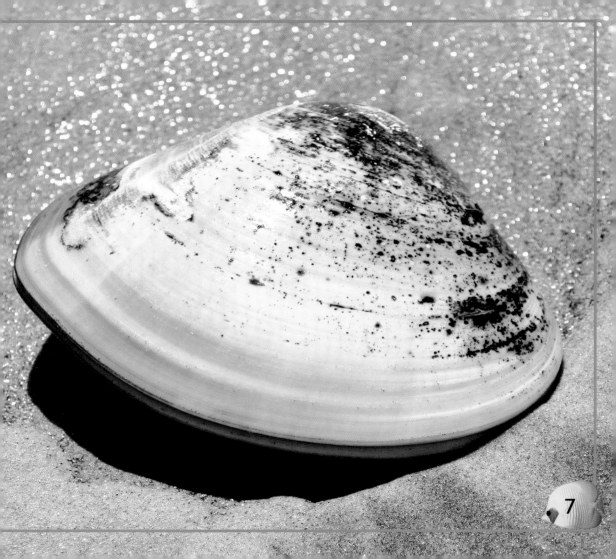

I see a crab.

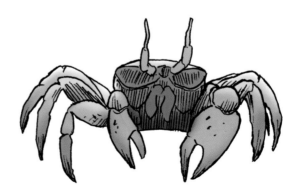

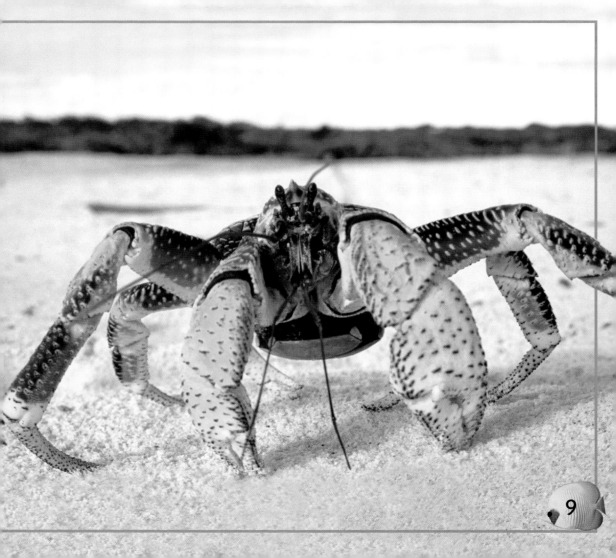

I see a fish.

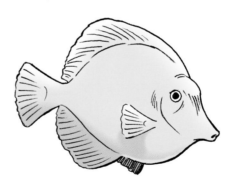

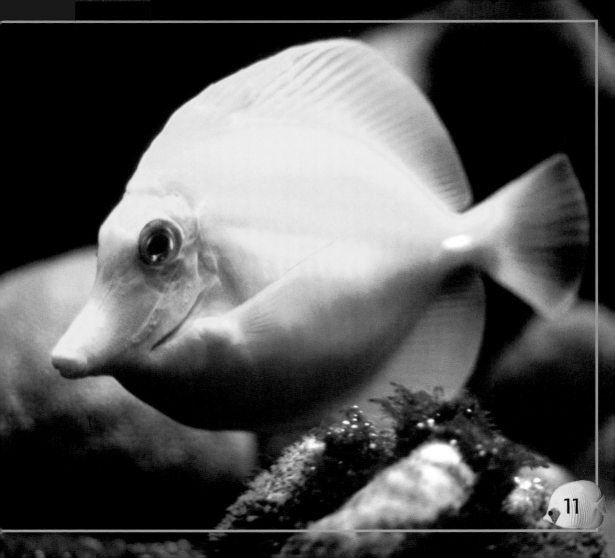

11

I see a seal.

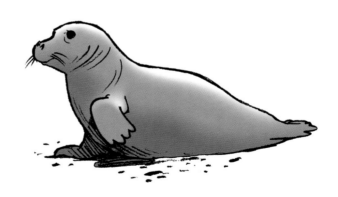

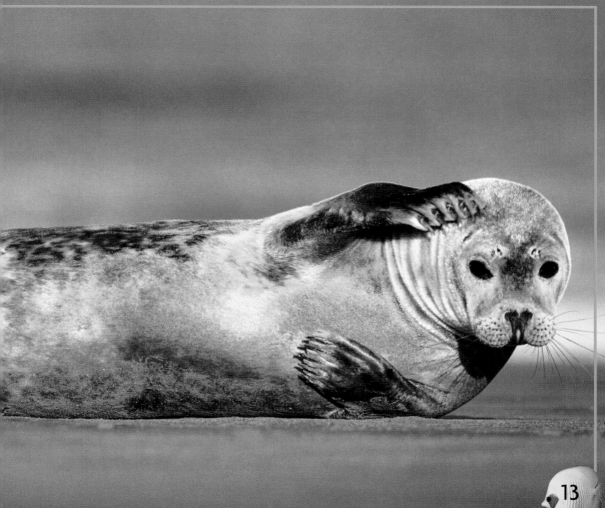

I see a bird.

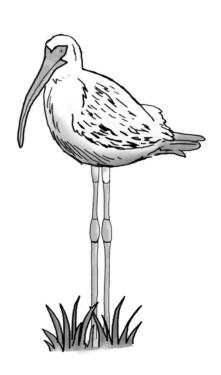

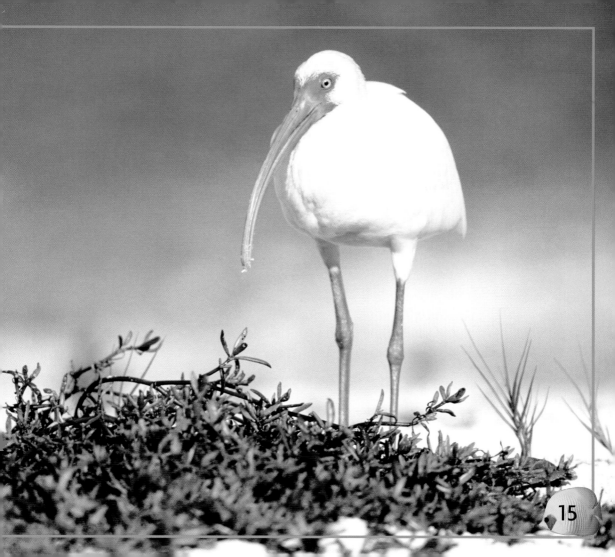

I see a beach.

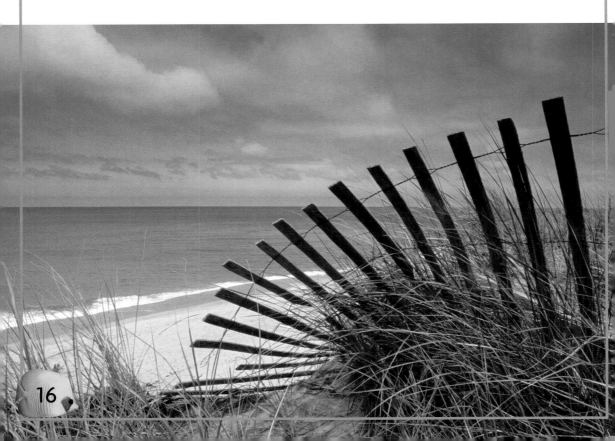